# LITTLE GUIDE TO BIG CHANGES

# THE LITTLE GUIDE TO BIG CHANGES

**6 Steps to Creating Lasting, Positive Change in Your Life**

## SARAH M. COLLINS

**GOOD TIMES BOOKS PVT. LTD.**
New Delhi (India)
www.goodtimesbooks.com

Published by
**GOOD TIMES BOOKS PVT. LTD.**
H-13, Bali Nagar, New Delhi-110 015 (INDIA)
Phones: +91-11-25913301, 45069086 *Fax:* +91-11-45069086
Email : info@goodtimesbooks.com
Website : www.goodtimesbooks.com

**First Good Times Edition 2011
Second Good Times Impression 2013**

ISBN-13 : 978-93-806191-3-2

Cataloging in Publication Data--DK
Courtesy: D.K. Agencies (P) Ltd.
<docinfo@dkagencies.com>

Collins, Sarah M.
　The little guide to big changes : 6 steps to creating lasting, positive change in your life / Sarah M. Collins.
　　p. cm.
　ISBN 9789380619132 (pbk.)

　　1. Self-help techniques. 2. Self-actualization (Psychology)　I. Title.

DDC 158.1　　22

Published in arrangement with
New Pathways Press
55 Mary Jones Road, Newton, N.J. 07860
Copyright © 2009 Sarah M. Collins
Poem "Transform" Copyright © 2009 Sarah M. Collins

No part of this book may be reproduced or utilized in any form or by any means, electronic or mechanical including photo-copying, recording or by any information storage and retrieval system, without permission in writing from the publishers.

Printed in India at
**Salasar Imaging Systems**

# Dedication

To seekers everywhere;
may you find and connect
with the limitless power
source residing within.

# Table of Contents

**Section One ~ Beginning...**
**One | Choose Change**
- Enliven Your Life through Conscious Change .. 17
- Launching the Process ............................ 19
- Taking Time for # 1 ................................ 21

**Section Two ~ Divine Guidance**
**Two | Speaking from the Heart**
- A Spiritual Perspective ........................... 27
- Your Special Lifeline .............................. 28
- Seeking a Connection ............................ 29
- Why Pray? ............................................ 32
- Anytime and Anywhere ......................... 33
- Heart Sense ......................................... 35
- Ask and You Shall Receive .................... 36
- The Significance of Reaffirming ............. 38
- Trust the Answers ................................ 39
- Acceptance and Faith ........................... 41
- Live the Way You Pray .......................... 42
- In-Sync ................................................ 44
- Joining with Others ............................... 45

**Three | Whispers of the One**
- Joining as One ..................................... 47
- Ways to Commune ............................... 49
- Preparation & Expectancy .................... 51

*The* LITTLE GUIDE *to* BIG CHANGES

Routine Matters ............................................. 53
Habitual Pursuits ........................................... 54
Steps Along the Way .................................... 55
   Chanting and Mantras ........................... 56
   Images ..................................................... 57
   Breathwork ............................................. 57
   Affirmations ........................................... 57
   Ideals ...................................................... 58
The Road to Bliss .......................................... 60
The Power to Change ................................... 62

## Section Three ~ Self-Guidance
## Four | Looking Within
Self-Awareness ............................................. 67
Peering into the Dark .................................... 69
Creative Channels ......................................... 70
   Thoughts and Emotions ......................... 71
   Words and Actions ................................. 73
   Introspection .......................................... 73

## Five | Seeing is Creating
The Inner Wellspring ..................................... 77
Imagination is Key ........................................ 78
Change Yourself, Change the World ............ 80
Heal Your Life from the Inside Out ............... 82
Dream the Impossible ................................... 84
Aim High ....................................................... 85

## Six | Life Approach
What's Your Positivity Quotient? ............ 87
Shifts in Perception ................................. 89
Declare Your Truth .................................. 91
The Acknowledgment Factor ................... 94
Erase All Doubt ....................................... 96

## Seven | Freedom is Yours
Forward Movement Always ...................... 99
Cause & Effect ....................................... 102
A Matter of Perspective .......................... 103
A Gift .................................................... 104
An Uplifting Effect ................................. 105
Coming to Terms with Human Frailties .... 106

## Section Four ~ Foraging in the Regions of Mind
## Eight | A Call to Action
The Time is Now .................................... 111
Self-Discovery: Questions & Answers ...... 112
More Paths Along the Way ..................... 116
   Journaling ......................................... 117
   Dream Solutions ................................ 118
   Guided Imagery ................................. 120
   Using Art ........................................... 122
   Self-Direction .................................... 123

Source Notes ........................................ 127
Recommended Readings ........................ 131
About the Author .................................. 133
Special Offers ....................................... 135

# Acknowledgments

Special thanks to my family for their patience, encouragement and never ending support of this project. Also for their help when I was at a loss for words, for being another pair of eyes in searching out manuscript errors and most of all for their prayers that it be completed on time.

And to everyone else who contributed to this work, whether it was reviewing a chapter or two or giving their opinions about specific aspects of the book, I sincerely thank you all!

# Disclaimers

The One Great Spirit, our source and maker is known by many names worldwide. This book acknowledges and uses some of these names. No disrespect is intended by the use of or omission of such names. The Divine, God, Universe, Spirit, the Presence and Creative Forces are the most common forms used in the book and as such are interchangeable. Additionally, the use of any name is not an endorsement of any one spiritual path.

The use of gender pronouns can create a challenging situation. When a single pronoun is preferred, *he* or *him* is used. This is not meant in any way to infer a preference; it is simply a matter of readability from the author's viewpoint.

This book is intended to be a source of education and information. It is meant to raise one's awareness of the many options available for living a happy, healthy life. Every effort has been made to provide clear and concise information; however, being fallible, mistakes may occur in content or typesetting.

Furthermore, this book is sold with the understanding that the publisher and author are not engaged in rendering psychological, spiritual, counseling or other professional services. If assistance is required, please seek the services of a competent professional.

The publisher and author shall in no way assume responsibility, be liable in any manner to any person or entity with respect to any loss, damage caused, or alleged to have been caused, directly or indirectly, by the information contained within this book.

# Transform

*Change yourself,
Change your life,
Change the world.*

# SECTION ONE

*Beginning...*

# ONE

# Choose Change

*"Things do not change; we change."*
Henry David Thoreau
1817-1862, US author

## Enliven Your Life through Conscious Change

Life is change personified. Changing means allowing new experiences into your life. People are so afraid of change—there's such comfort in familiarity. It's in the knowing. You don't have to guess what will happen because the behavior, yours or the people around you, is predictable. Even if it's unpleasant, there is still comfort in knowing what comes next. Change is scary and unpredictable. Better to be safe and miserable than to risk the unknown. You never know, things could turn out worse than they already are! Then again, your life could magically transform into one of joy and beauty.

In order to move forward in life, change must occur. Otherwise, life stagnates. It stops flowing. Think of the Tin Man in *The Wizard of Oz*. When he was rained on, he rusted and couldn't move any longer. Is that what your life has become—still and motionless? Don't despair. All you have to do is decide to take action, follow through and then watch the changes come into your life.

This *Little Guide* is all about the means of creating change when you feel stuck. You can't change other people, only yourself and your own situation. This means the very first step begins with you. In order to change what's outside of yourself, you first have to initiate change on the inside. This requires patience, persistence, courage and belief in yourself.

Long lasting change is not instantaneous; you don't take a pill and voilà, your symptoms disappear and you're a new person. Patience is a prerequisite.

If you don't have the fortitude to carry on despite the obstacles you encounter, you will not succeed. Remember, anything worthwhile requires persistence.

Are you able to swallow your fear and move forward, despite the uncertainty? Courage will be your ally as you take the plunge.

When doubts creep in and you begin to question

yourself, look within to find the original idea or thought behind your quest for change. This will renew your self-assurance, your trust, your very belief in yourself.

These four attributes will take you far along the path of change. There are many others that can help as well: hope, confidence, devotion, focus... the list is endless. As the path of change is unique to you, pick the attributes that are imbued within *your* being, that are *your* strengths, and play to them. It may be necessary as time goes by to develop those qualities that are lacking in yourself as well.

There are six techniques presented in *The Little Guide to Big Changes*. Some may resonate with you more than others may. Each technique can be done alone or in combination. The choice is yours. The more you employ the methods in concert with each other, the more change and growth will occur.

## Launching the Process

It is paramount that you establish a pattern in your life that includes the spiritual. Make it a daily habit. If you are serious about transforming your life, you must first acknowledge the spiritual side of life, and then seek some form of spiritual guidance within yourself. No one else can do this for you; it must come from within. For lasting change to transpire, each of us must find the inner strength to look honestly at our lives and then devise a plan to be implemented daily. Doing so consistently, a positive habit is formed.

Always remember, if things seem too hard, too overwhelming, *then ask for help*. Divinity is present every moment and in every space, within and without. All you have to do is *ask* for help, for guidance. Divinity does not interact with us without being invited. Our lives include the use of free will, therefore, for good or ill, we are left to our own devices. If you seek guidance from the Divine, you must ask for it! Long ago, Jesus said these words, "Ask and it will be given to you; seek and you will find; knock and the door will be opened to you." Your individual religious beliefs or lack thereof does not negate those words. They speak the truth for all, regardless of your personal beliefs.

When we get in touch with our spiritual side, we open up to a world of endless opportunities. Our perception shifts, allowing us more insight into who we really are and what we are truly capable of as human beings. We instigate change on our own behalf through inner growth. As we grow, awareness increases and we are not such a slave to our emotions; they evolve and we evolve. Then the miraculous happens! Our lives begin to fall into place and everything flows more harmoniously.

Working with the spiritual principles contained within the following pages, you will set the intention for transformation. This will allow an energy pattern of attraction to develop whereby you will bring into your life what your focus has been. Never forget, energy follows thought!

If you want to change one or many things about your life, take the first step on the path to transformation: make the commitment.

## Taking Time for # 1

Don't you owe it to yourself to live a fulfilling life, one that's inspiring and stimulating, free from monotony? All you have to do to change things is dedicate time to yourself day by day and you'll soon be on your way to living a gratifying life.

Each day we keep commitments to others: our family, friends, work and even strangers. There's someone missing from the mix: you. If you can't make time for yourself, how do you expect to have a happy life? If you're constantly doing for others with no time for yourself, where does that leave you? Eventually disappointed, saddened and frustrated.

Taking time out to nurture yourself will have such a positive impact. It will increase your self-worth, improve your mental outlook, raise your patience level, relax your mind and body, and on and on. But the trick is scheduling time for yourself the way you do for everyone and everything else in your life. Just by spending some time at the start or end of each day wholly dedicated to you is a terrific way to nourish your inner self. Time is the most precious commodity you have, so devoting some of it each day to *only* you is one of the nicest things you can do for yourself.

Establish a routine for getting in touch with your inner self. This will give you the dedication and commitment necessary to create the change you seek. A good way to begin each session is by reading something inspirational or using a breathing technique. Then begin practicing one or more of the methods provided in *The Little Guide*. Soon changes will come into your life, some so subtle you may not realize the difference until you stop, turn around and see how far you've come. This can be the case in relationships. All of a sudden, it dawns on you that things are different and when you look back, the realization sets in that things have gradually changed.

If you want to experience real growth in your life, you have to allow time to focus on what's worthwhile to you. Whatever you do within the scope of your everyday life has a ripple effect, touching the lives of those around you. Only by switching the focus to your inner world will you

One | Choose Change

begin to make lasting transformations to your outer world. Going within holds the key to without.

Why not make the commitment today to start changing your life?

# SECTION TWO

*Divine Guidance*

# Two

# Speaking from the Heart

*"Prayer is not an old woman's idle amusement. Properly understood and applied, it is the most potent instrument of action."*
Mahatma Gandhi
1869—1948, Indian leader

## A Spiritual Perspective

Prayer is a funny word. Mention it to someone and you're never sure of the reaction you'll get. It conjures up so many images: kneeling in a church, sitting in a synagogue, a child saying bedtime prayers, a devout Muslim prostrating toward Mecca during his daily ritual. Religious implications are what come to mind and for some, may elicit a negative reaction.

Another way of viewing prayer is from a spiritual perspective, without religious overtones. Spirituality evokes a broader, gentler and kinder approach towards the universe and issues of faith and belief than do most religions. It suggests tolerance and acceptance of differing viewpoints. Approaching prayer from a spiritual point of view makes it more inclusive. The attitude is more focused on the unity, the commonality and interconnectedness of all things. Whether speaking to God, Buddha, a saint, your angels, someone or even something else, adopting a spiritual perspective allows you the freedom to encompass a wide range of elements that compose and construct your unique spiritual path.

Spirituality is often viewed as seeking a more individual and personal relationship with the Divine. Today, religion in the West doesn't endorse taking a personal approach to God. Eastern religions however, favor and encourage this manner of seeking the Divine. A direct approach reaps many untold benefits: inner strength, confidence, guidance and happiness to name a few. Plus, there is no downside to a direct approach. Connecting with that special part of you that is greater than the sum of your elements is such a joyous and uplifting experience, it makes you glad to be alive.

## Your Special Lifeline

Seeking a connection with Divinity opens up a

## Two | Speaking from the Heart

pathway of inner guidance. Following its direction will never steer you down a wrong path. It is the most reliable resource you have because it is Divine in nature.

Prayer is one manner of seeking inner guidance. The ways in which your prayers are answered can be subtle and surprising. Prayers do not usually respond in an ordinary manner. However, seeking a connection with the spirit world through prayer is one expression of life that can be counted on, always.

Prayer is not the divine province of any one path; it is open to all regardless of faith or belief system. Prayer is universal. It can be utilized anytime, anywhere, by anyone. The beauty of prayer is that there is no right or wrong way.

If you haven't tried praying before, you are missing out on a simple method that can add so much richness to your life. Communing with the world of the invisible brings you closer to your true nature, which is spiritual in origin. Attuning to Spirit can open up a dazzling array of possibilities that will enliven and amaze you. This contact should be cultivated so it can blossom in your life; it can be your lifeline.

## Seeking a Connection

Since we are speaking from a spiritual standpoint, it is necessary to widen our definition of prayer. Prayer is not the one-sided conversation it appears to be. On the contrary, it consists of dialogue and an answer. Prayer is a conscious attempt to connect with the Universe. It is a way of communicating with the unseen realm. Prayer is talking, and then quietly attuning to your surroundings awaiting the answer — which often takes time, but it will come. Usually it is done silently, but it can be audible as in group prayer. You can speak to whomever or whatever you choose: God, your higher self, a spirit guide, a deceased relative, your body, a sunrise. You are limited only by your imagination and your belief system.

Many will be surprised to see your body and a sunrise listed as things to connect with through prayer. But we are not talking about prayer in a religious sense. This is from a spiritual perspective that is open-ended, not closed off like so many religious institutions. Just open your heart a little bit and venture forth into a new mind-frame. It's not blasphemous, it's merely different. Again, you are limited only by your beliefs.

According to David R. Hawkins, M.D., PhD, prayer increases the rate of healing. Suppose your body is injured and the healing process is slow. Talk to your body with reverence. Ask that all the cells work together harmoniously for the greater good to bring about a swift healing. Every part of your body, from your cells to your organs and bones, has a job to do keeping the body in homeostasis. The body's innate intelligence

## Two | Speaking from the Heart

will work with you if you talk to it and ask. The change that occurs is the answer you seek.

A prayer offered when gazing upon the beauty of a sunrise is a way of communing thanks for the exquisiteness and delight Nature provides. You're not asking for anything, just giving thanks as you would if you were to sit down to a plentiful meal. Pay attention, the light may suddenly become brighter — a wink if you will — the colors more vibrant or a bird might distract you as a way of acknowledgement.

Sometimes, a person close to you passes on, yet there is no closure. Maybe you didn't get a chance to say good-bye, maybe your last words were said in anger or maybe the death was very sudden. You can still speak to your loved one. Remember, death is just an illusion. Your essence never dies, merely changes form; only the body expires. We are all connected at every moment within and without time and space. Your loved one will get your message. Find a quiet spot and open your heart. Unburden yourself and send love along with your prayer. You will be doing yourself (and your loved one) a great service. Even though you are not looking for a response, your prayer is always acknowledged. Oftentimes it will surprise you, and many times, it will pass by unnoticed. Open up to the subtleties of life that are all around you. Learn the art of observation. Use your intuition, listen to your feelings and be aware!

## Why Pray?

There are many reasons to pray. Prayer can be the key to finding solace in your life, the means of seeking forgiveness, or the manner in which you find guidance in your life. It can also be the means to satisfy a desire, to absolve you from something you said or did, or simply to give thanks. Most often, it's a method of asking Spirit for help with life's problems, whether for yourself or another. People tend to pray when they're in trouble or have a desperate need for something. For many, it's when they've reached the end of the line and have nowhere else to turn. Why is it that prayer tends to be a last resort for so many?

Prayer should be the first thing you think of when your problems seem insurmountable. After all, there is only one thing you can count on in life — no, it's not your family or friends I'm sorry to say — it's Spirit. The Divine is with you every step of the way in your journey of life and is closer than the air you breathe. It is at your beck and call, ready to intervene if you will just take the simple step of asking. Spirit is your private counselor, always at the ready with a willing ear. But this magnificent part of you is hidden from your awareness, cut off from your conscious self. Most of us walk through life with blinders on, never being aware of the details. Tunnel vision is so limiting! If we would just learn to open our hearts and minds, we would catch a glimmer of the Divinity that lies beneath our human facade.

Whenever you have a need, prayer is just a heartbeat away. You never have to wait for it, it is available 24/7, every day of your life. It doesn't depend on the weather or the economy, the opinions of others, how much money you have, your religion or lack thereof, or even your character. It only depends upon your willingness to commune with the unseen world of Spirit. Speak and you shall be heard.

Pray when you're anxious or lonely. Pray when you're losing hope. Pray when you need a shoulder to cry on; your tears will be dried and a peaceful stillness will envelop your heart. Best of all, pray when you are grateful for something or someone. Showing gratitude through prayer is a wonderful way of appreciating all the little moments that make up your life. Recognizing the significance of someone or something, valuing the many opportunities and challenges you are presented with each day are wonderful lessons in humility. Being appreciative and respecting the smallness as well as the largeness in life can teach you so much about what's truly important.

## Anytime and Anywhere

When do you pray? Is it only during holidays or at every meal? At night before sleep? Maybe you only pray when there is a blue moon or some other rare cosmic event. Perhaps you only pray when you attend church or temple. Prayer is not confined to any special time or place. A prayer said in the woods among nature's creatures is equally effective as praying in church at a child's baptism. Spirit is everywhere and will hear you and respond regardless of your surroundings or when you open up a channel of communication.

Some people will feel more comfortable in a traditional religious setting while others will be quite content wherever they happen to find themselves. Many feel prayer is only appropriate at specific times. For example, you may think a meal is incomplete without the benefit of saying grace. Praying over your meal helps to raise the vibrations of the food you're about to consume. Others find praying at mealtime unnecessary. There are no right or wrong answers. It's about what feels right to you.

What *is* important is what you hold in your heart during your prayer. Energy follows thought, so surround your thoughts with the necessary emotion to convey your message. If you want to express gratitude for the wonderful meal set before you, *feel* the gratitude. Don't just state a platitude. If you're hurting and need comfort, emphasize that. A quiet calm will descend upon you, the sign your prayer has been heard and fulfilled.

## Two | Speaking from the Heart

# Heart Sense

Talking to the Divine is a marvelous technique for initiating change in your everyday life. All that is required is *sincerity* of your heartfelt emotions, the *belief* that your words are being heard and above all, *trust* that your prayers will be answered. The response may be in a different form than what you were expecting and not on your timetable, so *patience* is another factor.

Prayer isn't difficult. It just requires a genuine expression of your feelings. The emotion behind the prayer is the prime ingredient, just as it is with any thought. For example, when you say a prayer of thanks the effect may be fleeting and go unnoticed, but when praying for a loved one with a serious illness over many days or weeks, the response can be tremendous. The important thing to remember is that the Universe does respond to prayer.

Focus your thoughts, focus your energy. Don't recite a prayer while your attention is elsewhere, giving no thought as to what you're saying or reading. If you don't put energy (emotion) behind your prayer, then the prayer is an empty vessel containing no power. The result will be as a drop of water. Give your words meaning and the prayer energizes into a powerful vehicle for change. That is why there is so much power inherent in group prayer. The more people that come together for a common purpose in the form of prayer, the greater the result than if prayed for by only one or two individuals. Alone, the result will be as a cool, refreshing pool stretching far into the distance. When multitudes pray together, the result will be as vast as an ocean. Emotional depth is the trigger point. Meaning gives prayer power.

Pray not just with your emotions but with your whole being. Pray from your heart, with love. Let love saturate each prayer so it is offered with the highest intent. Work to purify your heart so your prayers can reflect this purity. The emotional component is then strengthened, adding creative power to the prayer.

## Ask and You Shall Receive

A prayer can be simple or elaborate. It can be as easy as a one-sentence plea or as grueling as an emotional outpouring for help. All forms of prayer are equally valid. Even though the emotional component greatly enhances the power of prayer and sometimes the timeliness of response, a gut-wrenching plea is not at all necessary. Just expressing what you want in a genuine way is all that's required. This in no way diminishes the power inherent in the prayer. Prayer can be delightfully simple and spontaneous; formality and ritual aren't required, though it's fine if that's your preference.

There is no need to find an official place of

## Two | Speaking from the Heart

worship, no need to wait for a holy day or religious holiday and no need to wait until you retire for the night. All that's needed is a natural impulse to connect with the Universe *at that moment*. Simply by asking for things to come into your life in a heartfelt way, opportunities open up in response. The intent is central to your prayer.

Don't ask for things in an offhand way but be sincere. If you want to find work you might ask, "Help me find a job as an accountant in a technical field." Or maybe you want to meet someone who shares your fondness for high-quality food so you say, "I'd like to have a friend who shares my love of gourmet food." Notice that the first example is actually more focused in its request. Finding employment that meets certain requirements verses finding someone, anyone who loves gourmet food, is the tougher challenge. Widen your requirement or better still, have none at all. A better appeal would be "Help me to find a job I will love." Maybe you don't *love* accounting and now's your opportunity to find something more compatible with your personality.

If you pay attention, the situation or person you want in your life will be presented to you. Sometimes, if it's a person, he shows up many times. Maybe you run into him consistently over a matter of weeks and it makes you wonder. Wake up your awareness; notice the little things in your life. Then act with confidence based on your newfound knowledge. The Universe will always work with you. Just remember not to get too specific so it has some room to maneuver. When you get too specific in your prayer request it can actually diminish the intended effect. If you put too many limitations as a condition of the prayer you will find it is not as effective. Being a bit more general in your request assures that the right response will come from your prayer. For example, if you ask for healing in a relationship don't ask that the other person change their behavior toward you or insist on other detailed stipulations. Perhaps *you* are the one that needs to change or both of you need to adjust certain behaviors. Don't presume to know what would be the best outcome.

## The Significance of Reaffirming

An important component of prayer is diligence. When you ask for something to come into your life, even when you see signs of it, don't make the mistake of stopping your prayers. You have to make sure the answer is delivered. How? By praying in a genuine spirit, *consistently*, until the answer materializes.

Repeating the same tired prayer over and over again for any length of time until you're emotionally drained is a waste of time and energy. The amount of time you spend on the prayer is

## Two | Speaking from the Heart

inconsequential. Reaffirming your request is all that is required to actualize the desired outcome. Its manifestation is assured and will develop more rapidly when this condition is met.

Asking in a genuine manner is all that's required to attract Spirit's attention. Once you ask for something, the way is opened and forces are put into motion that will bring about the desired change. All *you* have to do is continue to reaffirm the prayer until your objective is realized. Don't give up on prayer. Your intention and emotional strength will propel your request forward until the creative power is unleashed and reveals the outcome.

Prayers oftentimes are presents given to those we love and sometimes are even meant for ourselves. John Van Auken, Director of the Association for Research and Enlightenment (The A.R.E.) tells of an experience Edgar Cayce had. "Cayce once had a vision of a room filled with gift packages stacked to the ceiling. When he got a reading on this imagery, he was told that these were things that people stopped praying for. Their prayers had created them, but before they could be delivered, the prayers ended, and here they sat."

## Trust the Answers

Intuition is important when you're looking for a response to your prayer. Listen with your heart as well as your mind for any subtlety of expression. Learn to trust the answers you receive and don't be afraid to act based on that information. Remember that you are a spiritual being that slipped on a garment of flesh and bones to experience life in the physical. Your connection to the Divine is your birthright. Teach yourself to trust the connection. And watch as miracles big and small take root in your life.

Be open to the response by becoming more aware of your everyday environment. Notice seeming coincidences or synchronicities. They are a way to get your attention. In actuality, there is no such thing as coincidence. Nothing in life is left to chance. There is a purpose and order to everything. When something surprising or unexpected happens without the benefit of planning, take this as a sign that the answers you seek are vying for your attention. Are all of your six senses open and aware? Are you paying attention?

All things unfold within their own time. There is a perfect order within the grand design of the universe. You can't put time constraints or other requirements as a condition of prayer. You don't barter with Spirit, you cooperate, doing your part. If you won't put forth the effort to help yourself, why should Spirit intervene on your behalf? God helps those who help themselves.

Sometimes you don't recognize when your prayer has been answered. If you've been

## Two | Speaking from the Heart

searching for a reply to your supplication, you might want to reevaluate what you consider an appropriate response. Frequently, it's your preconceived notions that prevent you from seeing what's right in front of you.

Thinking that there can only be so many ways for an answer to occur places limits on the response. Many times it's a matter of expecting a certain outcome to take place and when it doesn't happen you assume your prayer wasn't answered. You just have to learn how to read the response. How? Be alert to anything and everything that comes your way. Try shifting your perspective by being receptive to new possibilities. Open up your awareness and see what's taking place around you. And never underestimate the creative power of the Universe!

## Acceptance and Faith

Edgar Cayce often said, "Why worry when you can pray?" Worry is so disruptive to the mind's balance and ultimately, the health of the body. When you have no control over a situation, worrying won't change it. All worry does is promote anxiety and stress. The answer lies in acceptance and letting go of your pseudo control. Making prayer an integral part of your life relinquishes the need to direct everything. When you hand over control to God, you know your life is safe. It's a very freeing experience. You get to stop trying to figure out how to manage difficult situations, you get to sleep peacefully at night because nothing's disturbing your state of mind and you can finally make time for that hobby you've been neglecting, just because you've been too distracted with worry. Worry is like a thief in the night that robs you of seemingly everything. Instead of worrying, your time can be better spent elsewhere, with your family and friends.

Practicing prayer allows you to slow down your life, taking time to tend to the important aspects of living. Anxiety and preoccupation can be put aside in favor of a strong faith and belief in the spiritual side of existence. With faith, there is trust, no proof required. Without faith, you will not act (pray). With belief, there is acceptance and certainty, but without belief, there is only doubt and hesitation. Prayer can be a consistent aid on the road of life if you would only learn to trust in the spiritual segment of life.

Everything is connected at the subtle layers of reality. When you pray, you acknowledge this part of life residing outside the material realm; you acknowledge the Divinity of all life.

## Live the Way You Pray

According to Cayce, you should live the way you pray. If you pray for peace, then live in a

## Two | Speaking from the Heart

peaceful manner. If you pray for love, live in a loving way, giving love to those you encounter. If you pray for joy, be joyous. If you pray for courage, be courageous. Whatever you pray for, *be* that. Accept that you receive whatever it is you pray for. Be it. Do it. Live it.

Remember to pray often. Pray as you go about your day. You can pray as you walk to class, sit at your computer or fix a meal. Praying doesn't require folded hands or kneeling in supplication. It just requires the right attitude and the desire to initiate contact with the spirit world.

When you encounter a difficulty, pray right then and there for a good resolution. Pray for small things. Pray for big things. Pray you find the joy and laughter in life. Pray for others, your loved ones and neighbors. Pray for strangers you see on the street or read about in the news. Pray for people you find difficult and especially, pray for your enemies. An enemy is simply someone whose perspective is 180 degrees from your own. Since we are all One within the invisible thread of life, an enemy is really just a reflection of some part of you. Mostly, remember to pray for yourself, for strength and courage as you go about your life. Ask that you develop qualities you lack, to eliminate undesirable traits, and for growth in your life.

# In-Sync

Prayer affects everything from people, plants and animals to hopeless causes and situations. Nothing is beyond the power of prayer. It's such an easy method of attunement and one so effective and full of impact. It can be your personal comforter in the face of an approaching storm and your anchor during rough seas. Making prayer a daily habit will bring you countless benefits: serenity, joy, good will, confidence and best of all, peace of mind. Spirit is creativity in motion so it's impossible to guess how and where its effects will be revealed. Suffice it to say it will be awe-inspiring!

Learning to be aware of the faint undercurrents running through your life is a process that will bring you more in tune with your spiritual side. Begin today those practices that will make you more sensitive and alert: proper diet and nutrition, meditation, introspection, being in nature, even prayer. Attune your body as well as your mind and emotions. Your life will change from the inside out. You will become a different person, one more in-sync with the world, seen and unseen.

Once you start perceiving the reality of the invisible world in your life and you become accustomed to it, you'll start to realize a very basic truth: the Universe provides what you need. Most of the time if you'd just get out of your own way you'd be able to see the certainty of this. Think about what you truly need to live: shelter, food, clothing, love, caring, human contact. If you're missing something here maybe you're the reason. Are you blocking it?

Ask for the things you want in life; the Universe provides what you need. If you feel you're lacking in some area, karma might be a factor. Whatever the reason, know that you have the power within you to start changing your circumstances, *beginning right this moment*. And what better way than through the use of prayer?

## Joining with Others

If prayer is an avenue you'd like to explore as a basis for changing your life, why not take it one step further and begin your own prayer circle? A gathering of like-minded people coming together once a week or so to pray for each other, your loved ones, your community and even the world is a great way to make a real difference. Pray for peace, for wellness, clarity — anything you deem important and relevant to the members. On days when you aren't together, perhaps you can arrange a common time when you come together in Spirit to continue the circle. Remember to structure your meetings in a way that meshes with your lifestyle and vision for the circle.

Another activity might be keeping a journal

of each gathering and as each prayer comes to fruition, take note of the way it manifested. Over time, you might see a useful pattern and the effects could be quite astonishing. It would be an interesting project to keep a record of things prayed for and their results.

There are many existing prayer circles. Some belong to traditional religious organizations while others are less defined. Why not add your energy, your circle to the mix?

## Three

# Whispers of the One

*"Meditation... helps self more than self can be aided in any other way."*
Edgar Cayce, Reading 3226-2
1877—1945, US psychic

## Joining as One

If prayer is talking to God, meditation is listening to God. Meditation is about going within to commune with your Source and Maker. It is attuning your spirit to the One Great Spirit through which all things are possible. Meditation is a spiritual discipline, the goal being realization of one's self and spiritual source through the silence within.

Used since ancient times for initiating spiritual growth, meditation offers a gradual progression in the development of one's consciousness. It's a tool for gaining clarity in all your endeavors. Whenever important changes come knocking in your life, your spiritual nature comes into focus. Since you're a spiritual creature choosing to manifest a physical existence, it seems logical that if you want to make the right changes you must connect with that portion of yourself that is greater than the sum of your human parts—your spiritual beingness. Then you can feel confident the choices you're making are the correct ones.

Listening and being receptive are the guiding principles for engaging in meditation. Stilling the body and the mind in order to commune with your Source affords you the opportunity to transcend ordinary, mundane reality for a brief time. It allows you to raise yourself up vibrationally to a higher level of consciousness where you may join with Spirit as One. There is no greater blessing afforded humanity then the joining with Spirit; it is transformative.

Meditation is the ideal path to self-discovery. You can explore the many levels of your being, gaining so much understanding. All the assistance and resources you will ever need can be found within. When you receive information in meditation, it is not with your physical ears. The hearing comes from within. You won't always receive answers, but with perseverance, that which you seek will become known. Life is learned from the inside out. Experiences are assimilated on an inner level allowing changes in habit and perception to occur. When the changes are of a positive nature, growth results.

## Ways to Commune

Meditation requires three things: patience, practice and perseverance. After sustained practice and as your perception grows, you will begin to notice many changes taking place. Your capacity for positive, life-affirming qualities increases and your responses to others change. Compassion, inner peace and finding joy in the little things of life take on new meaning while an openness with others develops resulting in better relationships. Greater concentration ensues and stress and tension are greatly reduced or even eliminated. Other benefits include greater strength mentally *and* physically, patience, clarity, calmness, more energy plus it disciplines the mind. Additionally, the natural outcome of consistent meditation practice is spiritual growth.

There are many different meditative practices in modern society using various techniques. The most popular seems to be guided meditation using imagery to focus your attention. These short meditations might be practiced up to a few times during the day. The goals can be very diverse. What's your objective? Is it to balance your emotions or gain clarity? Invoke the Law of

Attraction? Some guided meditations focus on relaxation and calming exercises, some focus on creating abundance in your life, while others focus on accenting one's spiritual nature. There's also walking meditation for those who find regular meditation difficult. This involves focused contemplation.

What's the difference between meditation and contemplation? Meditation is the deep concentration of the mind on just one thing, then removing the focus to enter the silence within. The intent of contemplation is to ponder something thoughtfully and deeply, reflecting on it over a lengthy time. You may wonder about something and want to observe it from all directions, giving it serious consideration. It might relate to spirituality, ways to improve yourself, concerns about a relationship or anything else that resonates with you.

It's possible to find a meditation for just about anything today. The Internet is a great place to conduct your own research and find just the kind of practice that suits you best. Delving into them is beyond the scope of this book. This book's meditation focus is on traditional ways. Even if you're more inclined to follow a modern path, there is relevant information in the following pages that applies equally to any modern technique.

The aim of traditional meditation is union with God. It is not about consciously being aware of your physical surroundings. Imagery is used only for focusing the mind. The practice of meditation awakens the creative impulse electrifying all three bodies (physical, psychic and noetic) through the raising of the Kundalini energy that lies coiled at the base of the spine. The spiritual centers of the body—the chakras—are activated with the releasing of this energy. The Edgar Cayce readings suggest the chakras correspond to the endocrine system in the physical body and that the glands of the body are gateways for spirit (and karma) to express itself. When there is a difficulty with one or more chakras, it indicates a state of disharmony in the spirit.

## Preparation & Expectancy

It's always a good idea to prepare for meditation by purifying yourself mentally and physically. This will help you to be receptive to the spiritual energies released during meditation. For example, bathing cleanses the body, eating the right foods, getting good nutrition, and drinking lots of water help to purify the body as well. Abstaining from drugs and other stimulants is advised and some say sexual restraint is called for. Ridding the body of any impurities will aid the flow of the Creative Forces during meditation.

There is a definite relationship between the body and mind. The mental attitude you hold as you are about to enter meditation is vitally important. There is a physical activity taking place through your imagination. What do you hold in your mind? What you imagine is the signal to set the spiritual energy in motion. That's why it's so important to enter meditation with a clean body, mind and heart.

Mental attitude, like good nutrition, works to keep the body balanced. Cleanse the mind through introspection. You don't want to meditate when you're angry because anger is a destructive emotion—a poison harming whatever is in its way. Empty out all obstacles that would be as barriers to the spiritualizing energy. If your heart is full of malice, envy or other negative emotions, it will only serve to foster the manifestation of negativity in your life. Remember, what you focus on, grows. Wait until you're in a positive mind frame before attempting to attune yourself spiritually. Attitude is everything where meditation is concerned.

Try not to go into meditation with any expectations. This can form an obstacle closing your inner self off to any contact. Plus, you won't be disappointed when what you expected doesn't happen. Anticipating a certain outcome can produce pressure and anxiety. Just go with the flow, allowing yourself the freedom of stillness, the freedom to just be. Open yourself to the experience at hand. If no signs are forthcoming, it doesn't mean anything is wrong; many times you won't receive any information when you meditate. Any attempt at meditation signals the activation of spiritual energy. Something occurs, even if it's not what you expect or think should happen, or are even aware of. Don't give up; persistence is essential for anyone who meditates.

## Routine Matters

Try to meditate before you sit down to a meal. It's not a good idea to meditate after eating a heavy serving of food; it's best to wait a couple of hours. Make sure you are in a place where you will not be disturbed. Reserving a small space exclusively for your meditation sessions is ideal. Somewhere you will not be bothered by outside distractions. Wear loose clothing so you won't feel restricted in any way. Be relaxed and sit comfortably, either on a chair or on the floor. You may sit cross-legged if this is your choice but it's not necessary. What is important is your posture. Your spine should be straight but not locked. Some people fold their hands in their lap, palms down; others rest their hands on their thighs, palms up. Do what is right for you.

Meditating regularly, at the same time each day not only develops self-discipline, but your spirit will anticipate your actions. Do it at the same time, the same place, every day. If need be, schedule an appointment with yourself. A certain type of life style develops when working on the self, one that strengthens your willpower and determination.

## Habitual Pursuits

Before beginning meditation, it's always a good idea to do some breathing exercises to help relax the body. It also sends a signal to the spiritual forces within that you are ready to commence some inner work.

Most people breathe in a very shallow manner. Try deep breathing from your abdomen, making the most of your diaphragm and see if you don't notice a difference in your body. Take a deep breath, beginning all the way down in your lower abdomen. Breathe in, feeling the air expand your belly as it rises and fills your chest cavity. Hold it for a few seconds and then exhale slowly, letting all of the air out of your lungs. Do this for a few minutes and when you're finished you should feel a distinct change in your body.

Edgar Cayce taught a head and neck exercise that's ideal to use in preparation for meditation. (It also holds the added benefits of being useful for some hearing and eye problems, as well as aiding the circulation in the head.) This technique helps to open up the energetic pathway so the Kundalini can rise unobstructed.

Bend the head forward so your chin almost touches your chest. Do this three times. Now bend the head backwards so you're looking up at the ceiling and you can feel a nice stretch in your neck. Do this three times. Next, bend your head towards your right shoulder, doing this three times. Then bend to the left shoulder, again doing it three times. Rotate your head to the right in a clockwise motion, three times. Now reverse it, rotating your head to the left in a counterclockwise motion. Do this three times as well. This exercise can be done in a sitting or standing position.

It's a good practice to begin and end your meditation with a prayer. Prayer is a nice way to align yourself mentally with the spiritual forces at the start of meditation. It helps to center yourself and set your purpose. Speak to God about whatever is uppermost in your mind. It might involve the nature of an affirmation or an ideal you use in your meditation. Prayer at the end can be one of thanks and devotion and may include the asking of a healing for you, a loved one, your country or even humanity. Just express whatever is in your heart.

## Steps Along the Way

The essentials of meditation include focusing the mind and connecting to the stillness within. Have you thought about what your focus will be?

The focus should quiet your thoughts and take you away from the constant inner chatter that can sometimes be deafening. It should have the ability to move you in the direction of the inner peace you seek. There are several tools to choose from. Will you use chanting or a mantra? An object or an image? An affirmation or an ideal? Or will you use your breathing to calm and still the mind?

You don't have to use the same method every time you meditate. Probably, you'll come to favor one or two methods over the others. However, if you like mixing it up from time to time, that's fine also. There's no right or wrong answer; it's what appeals to you.

## *Chanting and Mantras*

The repetition of chanting is conducive to focusing your attention. It produces a kind of hypnotic trance that has the power to remove your attention from your senses. Chanting involves a mantra and melody, not any kind of singing per se. Some spiritual paths liken it to a prayer. A mantra works the same way using a word, a phrase or a sound though it doesn't involve any kind of musicality. 'Om' is a popular sound mantra and works quickly to center the mind. Mantras and chanting can be done silently when meditating alone.

## Images

Visualizing an object such as a candle flame works well in focusing the mind as does concentrating on a personal image of devotion, for example, Buddha or Jesus. If using a devotional image you can chant the name of the adored one or concentrate solely on his essence or what he represents.

## Breathwork

Readying the body through the focused regulation of the breath is a very effective way to draw your attention inwards. This technique works especially well. Breathe in through you nostrils, hold for a few seconds, now exhale through your mouth. If you like, you can extend the timing by inhaling to a count of three or four, holding for the same count, then exhaling to another three or four count. If you breathe to a specific count, do it enough so that you can reach a point where the breath becomes natural, i.e. you're not counting anymore. However, you still want the breathing to be slow and rhythmic.

## Affirmations

Affirmations and ideals are two more techniques, similar in scope. They both can be used as a mantra though in the case of an ideal, it's even better to focus on the *essence* of the ideal.

An affirmation is a positive statement, though it's much more than a mere suggestion; it is a declaration or an assertion of truth. Affirming an attribute is a great way of strengthening self-esteem, particularly when used in meditation. Working with an affirmation in meditation helps the intended supposition to grow in your awareness. When you feel it has become a part of your consciousness, you can move on to another one. Some affirmations are devotional in nature; these aren't meant to be short-term stepping-stones. You can work with devotional statements over very long periods in order to build a bridge of love to the Divine.

## *Ideals*

What do you aspire to? What is your ideal? Whatever it is, it will enhance the consciousness that is being created through meditation. Meditating with the right purpose, the right ideal is vitally important. Every time you meditate, some advancement in attunement occurs. Whatever you want to build in your consciousness should be the focus, whether it's the particular qualities of a saint or other person of devotion, or universal qualities such as peace, inner strength, cooperation, humility and love. Your focus will direct your mind. Instead of focusing on a quality using a mantra, try centering your attention on the *awareness* or *essence* of the ideal. Using an ideal in your meditation can have profound results.

Ideals are principles you seek to make manifest in your life. They're a useful tool for anyone looking to better themselves. Ideals are not just for spiritual seekers. If you're serious about changing your life, they're the perfect instrument to fine-tune your inner nature so change can result in your outer world.

Edgar Cayce often spoke about the importance of ideals and that we all have physical, mental and spiritual ideals. For purposes of meditation, a spiritual ideal is best. Why? Because as Cayce said innumerable times, "Spirit is the life, mind is the builder and physical is the result." Meditating on an ideal will spur its growth in your life. You can add an affirmation to reflect the ideal and meditate on this as well.

First, you have to set your ideal. Remember, it's your *motivation*. What do you wish or hope for, what is your goal? This becomes your spiritual ideal. Suppose you desire peace in your life, so you choose this as your aspiration. How will you accomplish this?

The mental ideal is based on *developing* the objective in your life. How do you approach the concept of peace? List the qualities of peace: calmness, quiet, serenity, harmonious, peaceful. Your mental ideal would be one of these qualities that you ascribe to peace. Sometimes the spiritual and mental ideal are the same, for example you might choose peace or peaceful for the mental ideal.

How will you promote peace in your own life? The physical ideal involves *action*. What activities would encourage the use of peace? How about meditation or taking a walk in nature? Or singing a goodnight lullaby to a baby? Harmony could be your physical ideal.

It's important to come up with activities for your physical and mental ideals. List all the activities you can think of and then begin integrating them into your life, slowly so you're not overwhelmed. Use your time in meditation to reinforce your spiritual ideal, for example, using peace as your mantra.

Those standards you want to strengthen or even develop will change over the course of your life. There are so many to demonstrate within the human condition: kindness, generosity, friendliness, openness, beauty, joy, balance, flexibility, gentleness, forgiveness, patience, optimism and so on. Love is the ultimate ideal; all others are pieces of the cosmic puzzle that need to be perfected within one's being. The completed puzzle is the realization of unconditional love.

# The Road to Bliss

Once the prayer and exercises are finished and the focus is chosen, it's time to begin the meditation process. Bringing your attention to rest at the third eye signals to your spirit you are attempting to connect with your Source and Maker. With your eyes closed, raise your eyes up to the center of your forehead and shift your attention here. Physically focusing at the third eye may be uncomfortable at first, but with practice, the eyestrain will disappear.

Begin focusing your mind on your breathing, chanting, ideal or whatever way you have decided to use to calm the mind. Make a concerted effort to push away any thoughts that seek to distract you. Keep your focus on your chosen method. Once the outside distractions have dissipated, let go of your attention and bathe in the silence, letting it wash over you. (You're not thinking at this point in the meditation.) When thoughts interrupt and the mind begins to wander, bring back your attention with just a word from your affirmation (or whatever your focal point has been). Stay with the focus for a little bit, then release it and immerse yourself in the stillness once again. Just be with the silence, be still and receptive. Whenever distractions enter in, bring your focus back for a short while before going back into the silence deep within. Be persistent and over time you will find you're able to remain in the silence for longer periods. Distractions are particularly hard for beginners. That's why you have to be determined and persistent in your goal of self-awareness. It is a long road but the rewards are priceless.

Meditation is not about resting half asleep; you are fully awake and alert. You're just disconnecting from the outside world, from your senses. The removal of the distraction of the senses allows you to move deeper into the core of meditation, where much is discovered and revealed. Your inner awareness grows and can lead to what the Buddhists and Hindus call Samadhi, the realization of pure consciousness. This state is reserved for advanced meditators.

## The Power to Change

Meditation has the wherewithal to change your life through the unfolding of the creative, spiritual energies in directing the mind to manifest change in the physical, outer world. The creative impulse is awakened and released in meditation. Creativity comes in a myriad of forms and has the capacity to open up a new way of being, a new way of seeing the world. Growth makes this possible, propelling one forward in the attainment of the goal: self-realization.

Meditation is about listening, about being open to receiving. It harmonizes the body, mind and spirit. The power to change through meditation is life altering; it will help you find your connection to the One. Cultivating the spiritual side of life facilitates guidance through a connection with Spirit. All the assistance and resources you will ever need can be found within you.

Open your heart and mind to the unlimited possibilities of meditation. Your life will be enriched in countless ways. It can be difficult to tap into the Presence, hard to feel it and be immersed in it. But it is *always* present. There is a part of you that knows this, that remembers this — how it feels, its beauty, its healing presence, its love. But you have forgotten all of this. You think you are alone, but this is not true. You are only separated and disconnected from the Source. Meditation has the power to bring you closer to the Presence, to make it a viable part of your life and with this attunement comes change. Meditation refines and perfects your inner self so change can spread to your outer circumstances.

# SECTION THREE

*Self-Guidance*

# Four

# Looking Within

*"There's only one corner of the universe you can be certain of improving, and that's your own self."*
Aldous Huxley
1894—1963, English writer

## Self-Awareness

What radiates from your inner being? Is it love, unity, the power of positive thinking? Or is it negativity, discord and pessimism? Whatever you dwell on determines the tools you use to build your life. If you use love and cooperation to build your reality, it will be reflected back to you in your experiences. Similarly, if your personality is centered on negativity, your world won't be a very happy place to live.

Look within to that portion of yourself hidden far from the world and see if you recognize yourself. Be honest — what do you see? Take one sliver of your life, for instance, a typical way of reacting in a common situation. There are many circumstances that meet this criterion. How about when you're cut off in traffic? Or somebody is rude to you? Or a colleague tries to upstage you? What's your reaction? Do you see any possibility for improvement?

There are so many outwardly inconsequential reactions to ordinary events in everyday life. However, these apparently marginal responses are the key to your real self. These small pieces are the basis for who you are and where you are in the long journey of life.

Changing the seemingly small flaws in one's personality is just as important as working on the bigger pieces. By zeroing in on a lesser portion of the whole, progress can be made more quickly and it's not quite as daunting. When you take small steps and see improvement, it bolsters your sense of accomplishment and encourages you to continue.

Looking to your inner self to discover the real you is nothing short of transforming. Introspection is an excellent technique for accessing your hidden motives and real persona. It cuts through the facade you put on for the world's (and sometimes your own) benefit. It's an amazingly strong method for eliminating those stubborn character imperfections. Self-analysis is not a quick fix. It requires commitment, perseverance and self-discipline. An honest perception of your findings is also required, otherwise how can you make the necessary changes?

## Peering into the Dark

A method used for curtailing undesirable habits, introspection is perfect for initiating growth and inducing self-awareness. Many people aren't in touch with their inner nature and really don't know what lurks there. Looking within to the deepest parts of yourself can be a frightening proposition but if you want to get to the core of who you really are without any pretense getting in the way, it's a necessity.

Everyone has varying shades of darkness that can increase or diminish greatly at different points along the path of life. Put aside your fear of the unknown and brave the elements of your own subconscious by peering inside. Only then will you be able to remove your blinders and see yourself for who you truly are. The key is acknowledging the shadow parts of your personality and being willing to change the unattractive elements. Recognizing the secluded parts of your personality is the first step to self-awareness.

Everyone has flaws; it's what makes us human. In order to grow and evolve, change is necessary. Self-examination of your shortcomings and the consistent correction *on the inside, within the limitlessness of your own mind* will induce the changes you seek. Introspection allows you to see the truth of who you are—if you are honest with yourself. It also enables you to change the things you discover by replacing them with positive parameters. Seeds of blame transform into forgiveness, contrariness into cooperation, prejudice into tolerance, coldness into compassion, cruelty into kindness... There is no limit to what you may discover about yourself with introspection, and conversely, no limit to the changes you may initiate. Little by little, you'll begin to notice positive changes in your reactions to people and situations.

## Creative Channels

Through the creativity of your mind, you construct your personal world.

This is done through four channels that are conducive to self-reflection: words, thoughts, feelings and behaviors. Each means is inventive and artistic on such a grand scale you probably don't perceive the ingenuity all around and within you that exists for your sole benefit. Examining these four highly creative tools through reflection gives you the key to life; it allows you the chance to *change* your private world from hell to paradise or somewhere in the middle. (You always go in the direction of your choosing—and it's not always towards the light.) Keep in mind, your outer world reflects your inner world.

Who are you? Who do you want to be? What kind of personal environment do you want to create? Examining these four areas that define originality and creativity in physical existence will allow you to become aware of the importance of these matters we all tend to take for granted. Then you can initiate action that will produce change.

## *Thoughts and Emotions*

Thoughts and feelings don't come from the brain and their existence is separate from the physical brain. They are produced by the creative power of the mind and are as real as you are. According to the teachings of Dr. Stylianos Atteshlis (aka Daskalos), each thought and emotion creates an elemental also known as a thought form. Each elemental is projected according to the amount of energy given to it. The strength of this energy is based on the intensity of the desire associated with the emotion or thought. Daskalos further explains that thought forms can never be erased or destroyed. They can be dis-energized, but once created can never be eliminated. Thoughts and feelings have one purpose only: to fulfill their goal. And the goal is the thought or emotion itself.

If you get very angry with someone and wish

him harm, that elemental *will try to fulfill its objective*. The more the thought is expressed, the stronger the thought form becomes. The same holds true for the emotion behind the thought; it grows more potent with each articulation. Then one day the unthinkable happens — the elemental achieves its purpose. When the goal is fulfilled, it returns to you and once again will be projected out, this time with even greater energy. This cycle can recur several times.

Thoughts aren't things to be taken lightly and discarded carelessly. Thoughts are immensely powerful components of the mind as are emotions. These elementals are actually responsible for building your personality. Teachers since ancient times have always stressed the importance of monitoring your thoughts because the more energy in terms of repetition and feelings, the more quickly the manifestation of your creation.

How can you stop the cycle of projection and fulfillment when the thought forms are malevolent? Daskalos speaks of cleansing the personality with introspection, allowing you to change, to grow and evolve. Replacing negative thoughts daily with positive ones is the way to dis-energize the harmful ones. What you think and feel definitely has an impact in the world at large. These changes are projected out into your immediate environment, then spreads to affect the world.

## Four | Looking Within

### *Words and Actions*

You can't utter any words or take action without a thought. It may appear that the thought occurs simultaneously, but it really takes place a nanosecond before the behavior occurs or the words are spoken. Elementals are again instrumental in how we behave and what we say. Sometimes thought forms come together in a group for added measure. When this is the case, it is because our personality resonates and identifies with those group elementals. This is why when we are attempting to cleanse the personality through introspection we include words and behavior as two more areas of concern.

## Introspection

Introspection works to eliminate self-destructive tendencies by replacing them with positive habit patterns. These negative proclivities may have formed last year or during your last lifetime. *When* doesn't matter; what does matter is that you've been alerted to these precedents through self-examination and now is the time to do something about it.

What things should you examine? There are four main areas previously addressed: thoughts, words, feelings and actions.

A good rule of thumb is to examine yourself

everyday. If you're fearful of what you may find just remember the first thing is to adopt an attitude of compassion towards yourself, not judgment. This is vitally important. Being human, you're fallible. It's not realistic to expect perfection from yourself; making mistakes, learning from them and growing towards love is what life is about. If you were already perfected you wouldn't be here!

The best time for attempting introspection is when you retire for the night. That way, you can observe everything you've done for the entire day in word, deed, feeling and thought. When you come across something you shouldn't have said or a feeling that was inappropriate, address it right there. Supplant the original emotion or words with its positive counterpart. Then move on until you encounter something else that needs altering. Don't forget to include all thoughts and behaviors as well. Sometimes it's easiest to take them one at a time, viewing the day in terms of your emotions, then beginning again with your actions and so on. Always replace anything even remotely unconstructive or harmful with something positive. Eventually, you'll notice the positive reinforcements have evolved into positive habits.

Self-analysis doesn't take hours, only minutes. The more you practice it, the easier it will be. If you want to adjust your habits so your life will change you have to make a concerted effort.

FOUR | LOOKING WITHIN

Make it a regular practice in your life and soon enough, you'll see the rewards.

If you'd like to track your progress with introspection, there's a method that has gained popularity in recent years: journaling. Keeping a daily journal of your mental constructs — your thoughts, feelings and words, as well as your behavior — will give you tremendous insight. If you practice introspection faithfully each day, you'll see your progress through your journaling efforts.

What are you building with your thoughts, emotions, words and actions? How will you shape your world of today? Let go of the past, releasing the hold of all prior elementals, focus on today and tomorrow will take care of itself. Remember, an engaging life filled with happiness is a choice.*

---

*The method of introspection discussed in this chapter including the dialogue about elementals is based on the teachings of Dr. Stylianos Atteshlis (aka Daskalos). For more information, see the Notes section.

# Five

# Seeing is Creating

*"Imagination is more important than knowledge."*
Albert Einstein
*1879—1955, US scientist*

## The Inner Wellspring

The source for changing your life is a vital, inherent part of each human being. This inner wellspring never runs dry; it is constantly flowing. It is where your creativity originates, where the imagination resides. And it is powerful beyond measure. Divine in nature, it allows each of us to create our very lives.

Available day or night, it is accessible in the flash of a nanosecond. Conjuring a mental picture through the land of imagination, extracting a unique idea from the very ethers within, even forming our daily thoughts are all brought about by this source: the mind. Everything in creation consists of Mind.

Without this amazing resource, there would be no creativity and nothing would exist.

The mind (not the brain!) gives us the ability to visualize, to imagine, to build and create. We can literally build sand castles in the air (think skyscrapers) using our creative talents governed by our mind. Imagination is the tool given to us to actualize our creativity; it is humankind's greatest means of exploring the universe and all it contains. No wonder Einstein found it so appealing and even more essential than knowledge!

Imagination sets the artist loose on his chosen canvas: music, painting, writing, architecture, and even science, mathematics and technology. It is the fountainhead of creative power within the wellspring of the mind. Without imagination, humankind would fail to make any progress at all. This immensely valuable faculty is what gives life its distinctive and original quality.

## Imagination is Key

Life is a creative act manifested through imagination; it is an effect made possible by way of dreaming or visualizing. Nothing is beyond the realm of imagination. Its power is so great it has the ultimate ability to generate change at any moment on the continuum of existence.

So what does that mean for your life?

It means you have the power within you to

## Five | Seeing is Creating

shape your life any way you want. With a little effort, you can propel yourself out of your rut through the sheer force of visualization. And what a powerful force it is—it should not be underestimated! What do you want your life to be like? Do you consistently aim big or do you usually settle for your lot in life? We all have the power within us to change our life. Everyone has an inborn capacity to dream, to visualize. Even if you're one of those people more inclined towards an auditory or kinetic stimulus, the gift of visualization still resides within you. Sometimes, a little bit of practice is all it takes.

If you could live the life of your dreams, what would it look like? Visualize it in minute detail. That is the key: detail. When you use your imagination, nothing precludes you from having as much or as little detail as you deem necessary. As the dream weaver, you control all the elements. The more real you make the images in your mind, the clearer the mental construct and the more time devoted to visualizing, the faster the manifestation process works to actualize your dream.

You really are the creator of your destiny, your life. The words you speak, the feelings you have, the thoughts you think, the deeds you carry out, the dreams you dream, the attitudes you cultivate and the beliefs you have, all this produces the life you're living, moment by moment.

Everything begins with an idea. That idea

begins inside you. Nurture it and watch it grow. Visualize it. Dream it. See all the details in your reverie. Make it come to life in the same way a writer of fiction makes his stories come to life — by dreaming it into existence.

Take an idea you would like to explore with your imagination. Set aside five minutes of each day to focus exclusively on this idea. Build the idea in a dreamscape; clarify every detail as you would in storytelling. Eventually, you'll want to start to take action. This allows you to build your dream in the outer world. It's not necessary to finish constructing all the images before you begin to take action, but it makes it easier if you've developed a good foundation.

Dreams aren't stagnate, their very nature allows for expansion and revision. Just keep visualizing, keep building your life. Continuity is key. Before you know it, your dreams will begin to manifest and you'll be well on your way to living your ideal life.

John Anster, in his 1853 translation of Goethe's *Faust* said, "Whatever you can do, or dream you can do, begin it. Boldness has genius, power and magic in it."

Where will your dreams lead you?

# Change Yourself, Change the World

Changing your life doesn't just mean adding different elements; it also includes eliminating

## Five | Seeing is Creating

undesirable factors. Change all your experiences — situations, events and interactions with people — by altering what's already inside of you. Eventually, it will be projected out into the world. Purge yourself of objectionable habits to allow room for desirable elements to take shape. Visualize healthy attributes becoming part of your life. Become the person you've always wanted to be.

If you're in a bad marriage and want to save it but don't know what to do to change your situation, begin today to imagine a better life together. Visualize all of the elements that in your mind make for a good relationship. Do this continually over the weeks and months ahead. At the same time, you should focus on changing yourself instead of trying to change your spouse. Work on the difficult parts of your personality with the aid of visualization. See yourself as you would like to be. Include other methods such as introspection and prayer to support you in your quest. You just might find that your marriage begins to turn itself around.

Don't assume that all the problems with your marriage lie solely with the other person. Remember, it takes two to tango. Stop the faultfinding and center your attention on ways to improve how you interact in the relationship. Make the necessary changes to *yourself* and watch your spouse and even others in your life begin to react differently towards you. The only way to change your life is by changing *you*.

Relationships are central to everybody's life, so start applying this concept to any difficult relationship. Visualize how you would like your dealings with others to be and begin making it a reality. Everything you need, all the essential ingredients already exist. You just have to go within to start the creative process. Anything you create, from a sculpture to a baby or a special relationship takes time. Nobody said it would be easy or quick, but the rewards are beyond measure.

## Heal Your Life from the Inside Out

A very special quality associated with visualization is its capacity to heal. There are many avenues to healing but very few that can work on many levels: physical, mental, emotional and spiritual. Using your mind to construct powerful images and applying them as a focal point for the purpose of healing is unique to visualization. Whether you want to create a sound body or mind, visualization is a highly effective and potent means for altering your life.

Let's suppose that you're suffering from a debilitating disease like cancer. Picture in your mind a squadron of Jedi fighters shooting golden missiles at the cancer cells. As contact is made, the diseased cells explode in a golden-white light;

## Five | Seeing is Creating

all the cancerous tissues have been destroyed. All that remains is healthy, pink tissue. I like to use the colors gold and white because "gold is the true color of healing" and white is the color of purity (free from anything harmful) and wholeness (all colors combine to make white). Metaphysically, white is the highest vibration of all the colors.

Choose the scenario that works best for you. It might be a traditional battlefield or maybe an ancient one. You choose the setting, the players and the ammunition. You'll be most passionate when you decide upon the elements of the dreamscape. Make it as real as possible. Go to battle with your disease at least once a day, more if you can. And always see yourself as the victor. Don't stop visualizing until you are given a clean bill of health; even then, you may want to search out any potentially damaging cells from time to time and work your magic.

Another layer of the healing process is to project healing images to the infected areas. Bathe your diseased body part in liquid gold, believing that the curative powers that are the essence of the gold vibration will soothe and rebuild health in the damaged body parts. Blanket your body in the white light of protection, knowing no harm can come to it and knowing it is fully restored.

Many people have been successful visualizing their way to health. Will you join their ranks? After all, there's nothing to lose except your affliction.

Healing, no matter what level it occurs on, is instrumental to opening the doors to growth and change.

# Dream the Impossible

Anything you can imagine is within the scope of possibility. Anything at all. If you can think of it, it's possible. *Nothing* is within the realm of impossibility. You have to make your own magic. Dream the impossible dream. Make-believe isn't just for children anymore. Let your creativity empower you. Create the life you've always wanted using fantasy as the vehicle.

If you want to win Wimbledon or the Indy 500, be a great soccer player or NBA star, dream your way to the championships. See yourself before each event playing a spot-on game. Rehearse it in your mind repeatedly until the big day. It can be even more effective than physically training. Practicing with your mind is a powerful technique that can propel you to the heights of your game.

All the great actors use visualization, probably without thinking about it. They rehearse their lines and literally become their characters. That's why they're believable. Lesser actors don't seem to get so involved in the process.

Another great use is for visualizing the outcome of a stressful situation: a job interview, taking a test, going up against the school bully. Children

## Five | Seeing is Creating

seem to be especially adept at dreaming. What better way to teach the virtues of non-violence in the schoolyard than with visualization? There are innumerable situations where visualizing can have dramatic results.

What do your daydreams look like? Are they simple or elaborate? Are they centered on material desires or life's intangibles? What inspires your dreams? Creating a vision is the first step on the road to manifestation.

## Aim High

Whatever you desire in life or wish your life could be, start moving your life in that direction. Begin by asking for what you want and then start picturing it in your mind. Color it with intent and feeling. Intention is so important because it can help propel your idea along the winds of change. It can be the sail that catches a strong breeze, hurling you toward your future.

What's your goal? Is it only about you or does it include others? Selfishness can be your undoing, so tread carefully here. It's ok to want things for yourself, that's just human nature. But if your dreaming activities begin to take on a greedy element, watch out! The whip of karma can be very unpleasant. Visions of power and wealth can take on a very seductive and dangerous quality. Be careful what you wish for! When God blesses you with abundant financial resources, there's always an element of responsibility that goes along with it. Will you use it only for yourself or will you brighten the lives of others as well? Remake your life in a purposeful manner with others in mind and living will take on a joyous tone. The effects, the karma will be pleasant as well.

Given its potential, visualization can be an immense source of help in your search for change. The trick is to be persistent and consistent with the details. Should any part of the manifestation not be all you had hoped for, simply amend your vision by fine-tuning it. There are so many ways to use your imagination to transform your life. What ways can you think of? Start dreaming your way to happiness with the life you want and deserve!

# Six

# Life Approach

*"The measure of mental health is the disposition to find good everywhere."*
Ralph Waldo Emerson
1803 — 1882, US essayist & poet

## What's Your Positivity Quotient?

Ultimately, how you approach life all comes down to personality and how you interact with existence. The multiple variables of childhood environment, experiences with school and other authority figures, your friends and family relationships, and of course the ancestral DNA passed along through the generations to the lucky recipient — you, are merely props designed to propel you forward along life's continuum to self-realization and enlightenment.

The role you play in life is hard-wired to your life lessons. The totality of your persona and its interplay with cultural orientation, race, religious leanings and socio-economic level is designed for you to get the most out of your life lessons. All the details are chosen with this objective in mind.

Personality is really the only major variance between people (the other details being supporting elements) and this is the one factor that affects how you react to life and the subsequent karma that follows. The sum of your individual traits determines your whole approach to life, your perspectives and perceptions.

With this in mind, each person can assess his affinity for positivity. Personality will determine your inclination for happiness vs. sorrow, positivity vs. negativity. Looking over your life with the benefit of introspection can help you discover your positivity quotient. If you find it lacking a bit, there are ways to enhance the positive potential in your life. Attitude and gratitude, affirming, belief and faith all can contribute to a healthy, positive state of mind.

Repeated attempts at positivity will help you to grow in awareness and transform your consciousness. Drive out the negative and expand the positive by developing worthy behavior patterns. The seed planted today will eventually mature and become a driving force within you.

Six | Life Approach

## Shifts in Perception

Attitude is everything. It affects how you react to life and is a measure of happiness. When you see a glass partially filled, do you view it as half-full or half-empty? Your answer will determine your general approach to life. If it's half-full, you tend toward a positive, optimistic outlook. Your worldview will probably be encouraging, hopeful and brimming with confidence. You no doubt come across as upbeat, with a sunny disposition. Should you see the glass as half-empty, you're more likely a bit pessimistic about life. A somewhat subdued, more passive and perhaps indifferent attitude might be typical.\*

Where do you fit in? It's important that you get in touch with your basic nature. In order to make changes, you have to know the fundamental energy that drives your life.

It may be that your outlook on life needs some adjustment to loosen the glue that binds you to stagnation. If your glass is half-empty or chronic negativity plagues you — from lasting unhappiness, discouragement or other negative feelings, to any kind of invalidation or withdrawal from life — your attitude needs to be addressed. The likelihood of falling back into familiar, yet idle and unproductive patterns

---

\*These are highly generalized descriptions of two opposite perspectives; most people will undoubtedly fit somewhere between the two extremes.

89

will be diminished as you openly address your attitude on a consistent basis.

There are attitudes about all sorts of things: work, family, school, people you encounter everyday. Your personal viewpoint is front and center in every situation. You can display an arrogant or humble attitude, one that's helpful or uncooperative, and a multitude of other positive or negative qualities to exhibit. Attitude accounts for how you feel about absolutely everything in life. It also has the unique ability to determine your level of happiness. Attitude and emotions are intimately connected. Yet, a slight adjustment can make all the difference. Attitude is your window to the world. Is your window filled with sunlight or gloomy shadows? Shift your attitude and the view from your window will change; your emotions will change as well.

Try this simple experiment. The next time you encounter a difficult person (it doesn't have to be a stranger, your family will do nicely), instead of *re-*acting to him or her, try taking a step back and adjusting your own attitude. Instead of reacting negatively, try adopting a neutral stance. Apply this to every level: your words, your body language, and even to your thoughts and feelings. Extend this idea to your actions if necessary. Compel yourself to shift your perspective from your usual way of interacting to a position of neutrality. By not responding to the other person's discordant energy with more discordant energy, by taking a different approach, *i.e. a different attitude*, you are throwing water on the fire instead of fanning the flames.

It really isn't as difficult as it might seem. Purposely slow down the emotion of the moment by taking a long, deep breath or two and then change how *you* react and watch what happens. The distressing energy dissipates; it has nothing to connect with. Opposites always repel and disperse.

The more you practice this, the easier it becomes. And every time you apply this concept, you're developing this behavior into a habit. Soon it will become second nature to you. But that's not all. You can apply this idea to any kind of situation or circumstance you encounter. You can change your attitude anytime it's needed. It really is possible to lead a happy and harmonious life.

Here's something else you might try. Make an effort to act only out of love for one day. If that's too daunting a task, try it for one hour. See how your world transforms itself. Develop it to the point where it becomes second nature to you.

Remember, what begins on the inside eventually manifests outward.

# Declare Your Truth

Affirmations are a terrific way to increase your positivity quotient. As a strong statement expressed wholeheartedly, it has the ability to reprogram the subconscious with the aid of repetition. The subconscious doesn't edit, it works based on what you think and believe; it reacts to conviction. For example, if you generally view people as friendly and accommodating that will be your usual experience. However, if you assume the world is a scary and awful place that is exactly what you'll encounter. Your life mirrors your beliefs.

An affirmation's primary aim is to evoke positive change in a person. It's a method to train your mind to adapt to a particular way of thinking and becoming. When you express a new way of thinking with confidence and certainty, over time you will change your subconscious. If you tend toward a more pessimistic view of life, affirming a more optimistic outlook will eventually result in a more constructive and positive approach to all your endeavors. Change your thinking and consequently your beliefs, through affirmations.

Make a list of affirmations you'd like to implement. Writing them down helps to commit to them as well as bring them to fruition. Noting your reaction to each statement can also assist you in applying them. If you feel especially timid toward one because it's out of character for you, identifying your true feelings can boost your determination to make the necessary change.

Practice your affirmations everyday. Say or read them aloud. Infuse your consciousness with their essence. You can make a recording of them to use while you're driving, walking the dog, when you're gardening, doing household chores, running on the treadmill, or even as you're about to fall asleep. Another way to use an affirmation is during your meditations as previously discussed. If you're performing a menial task you can also implement a visualization exercise along with the affirmation for added emphasis. But don't try this while you're driving!

The emotional component greatly affects the results you'll achieve using an affirmation. Remember, it's the sentiment that propels it to bear fruit. If there's no feeling behind the words its effectiveness is lost. With no emotional connection, there's only an empty vessel (a thought) lying idle on the sea waiting for the wind (sentiment) to propel it toward a distant shore (its goal). The emotional undercurrent is part of the very fabric of each affirmation.

The other factor that affects the outcome is your belief system. If you don't believe in your affirmation 100%, it will ultimately fizzle just like a failed firecracker. A strong and firm belief is needed to bring about a change in your state of mind. Saying you're a good salesperson but without the necessary belief, won't get you very far. Achieving the truth of the statement is what will yield results.

Affirmations are a way to aid and change the

mental activities. They bring new ways of being, of acting, of thinking, of feeling to one's life. By its very nature, an affirmation is a positive assertion of truth and commitment to a desired goal.

## The Acknowledgment Factor

Life is about change, and sometimes those changes have a way of sneaking up on us. You always think, "If I had some warning of what was to come, I could have prepared myself." But humans are stubborn creatures and don't normally make a habit of letting go easily. Learn to embrace change and let go; don't dwell on the past — the present moment is all you have. Make the most of it. Take up all the tools at your disposal and begin right now to shape the life you want to live. And remember to be grateful each step of the way. Life can change on a dime. Count all your blessings and opportunities, and remember to include all the roadblocks and challenges. Learn to value what you have, when you have it.

Develop an attitude of gratitude. Make it a habit, preferably an everyday occurrence. Appreciate and take joy in the little things in life — they can be the most meaningful. One of the biggest errors in life is taking things for granted. They can suddenly be taken away. Things never stay the same. When something or someone departs from your life that you've taken for granted, often there's an emptiness that accompanies the departure. Learn to feel gratitude for what you have and then if it's yanked away it won't be so painful. Plus, as an added bonus, you'll have pleasant memories to cherish because you stopped to smell the roses and appreciated what you had.

Simplify your life so the demands and stresses of everyday are greatly reduced and maybe even eliminated. Simplicity can be an enormous help when you have to face a difficulty beyond your control such as the loss of a job, a home, even a loved one. Focusing on what you truly value instead of what you've lost will move your attention to *all you have*. Remember the good things and you'll develop a new appreciation for all the blessings in your life.

In situations of great loss it can be therapeutic to write down what you're grateful for and why. It can really put things in proper perspective. But don't wait for tragedy to strike. Start today to value what's important. Be sincere. If the feeling doesn't grab you, move on to something more significant. Express your thanks when it's heartfelt. Keeping a record of your gratitude can be a good reminder when you're just not feeling it. Spending time appreciating the details of your life on a frequent basis can promote a sense of calm and self-assurance. During times of reflection, give thanks for all you have in life and even for the things you don't have. What one person considers a treasure may be a burden for someone else. Most of all, be grateful for your relationships, especially the difficult ones because those are the ones that provide the greatest lessons. After all, isn't that why we're here on planet Earth, to learn lessons of love?

Your positivity level will definitely increase if you make gratitude an integral part of your everyday life. It's a wonderful virtue to nurture and watch as it grows. People, things and situations are put into proper perspective and cherished as the gems they truly are, not taken for granted and forgotten. If you're someone who has trouble feeling a sense of gratitude, try adding it as an affirmation or ideal to your meditation and watch what unfolds.

## Erase All Doubt

Placing limits on things, people or even yourself can be rather risky; you don't allow yourself the chance to see all the possibilities in life. Limits only serve one purpose: to place barriers in your path. When you limit yourself, you erect a wall between yourself and your objective. And no matter how hard you try to get around it, that wall just keeps getting taller, wider, and more impenetrable by the minute. If you think you can't do something, then right there you've stopped yourself; you've

## Six | Life Approach

placed a major roadblock in your path.

Faith and belief can be powerful motivators. Believing in yourself ushers in an awareness that can literally transform how you think about and see your life. You can be anything you want, achieve anything you can dream about. Your life can be exactly what you want it to be. There are no limits except the ones you place on yourself. Adopting an inner acceptance and optimism based on belief and faith is absolutely essential to anything you want to realize in your life.

When doubts creep in, reach down deep — there you'll find the resources you need to overcome anything in life. Don't look to others for the answers, look within yourself. Trust in yourself and have faith in your abilities. Act with courage and conviction. No one knows better than you what is right and best for you. Search inside yourself and you will always find your answers.

When you stumble, don't let disbelief destroy all you have built. Continue down your path with your eyes wide open, learn from your difficulty and move on. Maybe next time you'll have to search a little harder, but each time your self-confidence will increase and so will your self-reliance. Little by little, doubt will become a distant marker. Learn to depend on the forces within you; stop relying on what's outside of you — it's illusionary.

When you acquire belief and faith in yourself, you free yourself from crushing doubt. It bolsters you to action; it enables you to become proactive. You begin to exude confidence. Your self-esteem grows. You're finally able to look at life as a grand adventure to be experienced, not something to hide from in some self-imposed exile. Letting go of insecurities encourages optimism to grow.

Beliefs shape your world. Everything you think, feel and say, how you view people and how you react to them are all based on your beliefs. What is it you want to find in your life — happiness, companionship, wealth, adventure? Change your beliefs and know that they will show you the way to discover your fondest dreams. If you want adventure, believe you will find it and before you know it, the path will open up for you. Life is one giant miracle in action. Will you be a part of it or stay on the sidelines? Have faith and begin to walk in the direction of your dreams.

## Seven

# Freedom is Yours

*"Life is an adventure in forgiveness."*
Norman Cousins
1915—1990, US editor & essayist

## Forward Movement Always

Permanence is an illusion. Change is all around us—it's called life. Life is motion and it flows continuously; it is not still and unmoving. A state of change is life's natural environment. Even though you may consciously resist the idea of change, it is a state you engage in at all times, though perhaps unknowingly or better yet, not purposely.

At any given moment in your life, you are moving toward or away from something. It is impossible for your life to be immobile, frozen or static. This goes against nature. So no matter what you do today, choices are being made. Even when you choose to do nothing, that is a choice—moving you along your path, either toward or away from your goal, your very purpose for being here. Sometimes we end up taking a detour, taking us far from our intended destination. But the beauty of life is that mistakes can always be corrected, for life is continuous and merely changes form. We can always jump back on the main thoroughfare and get back on track. By taking a detour, we may miss critical signposts intended to support us on our journey, or we just might end up taking a shortcut. Shortcuts should always be approached with caution, as vital steps may be overlooked. It's best to travel along the main path so nothing of importance goes by unnoticed.

Oftentimes we chain ourselves to the past, rather unwittingly. This form of rebellion causes us to retreat along our pathway into what we think is a comfort zone. Refusing to forgive someone is a prime example. It literally keeps us in bondage and moves us away from our objective. The soul's intention is forward movement through our life lessons. Blame and the inability to forgive, no matter the reason, does not allow us to move ahead. Blame promotes stagnation (failure to progress) and is a burden we keep all to ourselves. It lulls us into a false sense of security, insisting that what we *feel* is right and just: "She doesn't *deserve* my forgiveness after what she did!" Yet, it is this very attitude that impedes our progress.

When we hold someone accountable for a

## Seven | Freedom is Yours

lapse in judgment or some form of wrongdoing, resentment is a natural consequence. The longer the aggrieved feeling is sustained, chances are the resentment will escalate into bitterness. This negativity will permeate the spirit, poisoning not only the relationship with the offender, but quite possibly other close relationships as well. Negativity has a way of seeping into everything it contacts; its very nature is insidious. The stronger the ill will, the more damage it causes.

Resentment, anger, jealousy — these are all closet emotions we try to hide from the world. These and other damaging emotions keep us from moving forward and keep our mind stuck in the past. Refusing to forgive can also set up harmful physical reactions as well. According to the twentieth century seer Edgar Cayce, holding onto resentment sets up conditions in the body that can cause cancer. It is important to note that physical illness can have an underlying mental or spiritual cause; not all illness is the result of physical distress. Dr. Kenneth Y. and Lisa V. Davis, co-founders of Natural Force Healing® also espouse this concept.

Recognize that the past offense cannot hold any power over you except the power you give it, the power you *allow* to dominate in your life. Hatred. Bitterness. Contempt. Dwelling on these and other negative emotions is not punishing the offender, it is punishing *you*. Harmful emotions create a breakdown in body, mind and spirit. Refusing to forgive someone is the antithesis to health and well-being.

## Cause & Effect

There is another consequence of refusing to forgive: karma. For those of you not comfortable with the word and its connotations, try substituting its equivalent from physics: the law of cause and effect. This law says that for every action there will be an effect. Actually, an action doesn't have to be a deed per se, but can be a word, behavior, feeling or even a thought. Thoughts are indeed things, feelings can be palpable, words can injure or heal and all behaviors produce an outcome. This is where physics and karma part company. However, if you think deeply on this issue you will see that karma encompasses *all* states of human affairs — nothing is immune.

Unlike the scientific law of cause and effect, karma builds up. It does not usually produce an instant effect, but can manifest later in life or even in another lifetime. Also, karma is neutral in itself; there is no good or bad karma. *Your actions* are what determine whether the effects will be pleasant or unpleasant. Forgiving another will have a positive result, while continuing to condemn someone for a failure in judgment will have negative repercussions. The very act of recrimination has so many ramifications: the words that wound; the intensity of negative thoughts and feelings; the resulting behavior(s) toward the person who offended you; and the physical, mental and spiritual effects of these actions. Now can you see why turning your back on forgiveness has such grave consequences?

## A Matter of Perspective

Learn to let go of petty animosities. Don't sweat the small stuff that's a natural outgrowth of living. Being human means we will hurt someone many times throughout our life and be on the receiving end of hurt feelings as well. The only way to end the cycle of emotional wounding is by growing so much in awareness that this type of behavior is not part of our consciousness anymore. Then the emotional cuttings will not have the power to injure us because *our perspective* will be different.

Oftentimes, the perceived offense has no basis in truth; it is only a belief based upon perception that is often flawed. Perception is what makes people different from one another. Humanity is like a multifaceted diamond radiating a myriad of colors, where each color is an individual perspective. It's easy to misread someone's point of view; misunderstandings happen all the time. Our hurt feelings are often based upon a faulty assessment: a certain look, a false impression, a misinterpretation, a difference of opinion, a mix-up, an argument or a misunderstanding.

Everyone has shortcomings and everyone makes mistakes. No one likes to be misunderstood. So why would you hang onto a grievance that may or may not contain an element of truth? Even if your appraisal of the situation were correct, why would you condemn someone for his or her actions? We are all fallible. *Blame the behavior, not the person.* The offending behavior is a reflection of their beliefs and attitudes. You don't have to understand someone's behavior, but at the same time, don't condemn him or her because of it either. Learn to look past the outer manifestation and see the inner potentials of a fellow spiritual being. Look inside at their spiritual essence, who they really are and learn to forgive. Seek compassion in yourself before condemning another. As we are all connected on a subtle level and we are all One, condemning someone is akin to condemning yourself.

# A Gift

It takes more energy to hold onto perceived hurts then to release them. Unlocking the chain that keeps you bound to your hurt and releasing yourself from your self-imposed prison is a gift you can give yourself. Through the act of forgiveness, you liberate yourself from the pain of hostility, jealousy, even hatred that lays heavy like a brick at the bottom of your heart. Forgive and poof! All that negativity vanishes like the wind, and you are free. True freedom is so special and precious, something no one else in the world can give to you; it can only come from within. Not only does forgiveness heal the wounds between people, it presents you with an offering of freedom. Forgiveness is truly miraculous!

## An Uplifting Effect

Take a long look at your life. Is it sweet and fruitful or bitter with resentment? Do you nurture forgiveness in your life? If not, why not?

Forgiveness is a lesson in acceptance and grace. Embracing these qualities creates a change of attitude resulting in a positive mental state that extends into all life areas. Positive emotions have a healthy, uplifting effect on the body. Forgiveness encourages constructive and favorable benefits for the *whole* person and allows you the freedom to move forward with your life.

So many people today need emotional healing. Just look at all the failed relationships, divorces, children being shuttled between two families, lack of family cohesiveness and loyalty. Not so very long ago, people stayed together, divorce was not common, the threads in a child's life didn't come unwoven so easily and the idea of family as a unit was an important and meaningful concept. It seems that people have lost their connection with timeless principles such as forgiveness. How many relationships would still be intact if forgiveness were freely given? Forgiveness comes in a small package yet its effects are enormous. It is the healing solution to so many problems in life. Forgiveness releases you from debilitating emotions, transforming your relationships. It is a simple tenet, but one that holds much power; forgiveness cleanses the soul.

## Coming to Terms with Human Frailties

Do you routinely forgive yourself? If you can't forgive yourself, how can you find it within you to forgive another? It's vitally important to let go of your own failures and shortcomings, to accept your own imperfections, to learn forgiveness for yourself. Otherwise, the dreaded stagnation sets in, once again chaining you to the past. You're human, you make mistakes. Resolve to do better next time. Life is about learning to do the right thing, the emphasis on *learning*.

Oftentimes, writing things down gives a new perspective and aids in finding solutions to problems. Write down all the reasons why you can't forgive yourself or someone else. Then write down why you *should* forgive. Now look at your reasons side-by-side and read them aloud. The

SEVEN | FREEDOM IS YOURS

original basis for holding onto a hurt won't seem as weighty as you move toward acceptance, and sometimes, it will even border on the ridiculous!

If you're still finding it difficult to forgive, reciting the Forgiveness Prayer below is a wonderful tool you can use daily, and in time, you will see a noticeable difference. Use it to heal relationships, situations, the past, whatever needs forgiveness. This prayer was written by Dr. Kenneth Y. Davis of Davis Advanced Health System and co-founder of Natural Force Healing®, printed here with permission.

### Forgiveness Prayer

*Please God, give me the strength and the ability to find forgiveness in my heart for all those I feel have wounded, offended or hurt me in the past or the present.*

Use the writing exercise and the forgiveness prayer to liberate yourself from the negative and often volatile emotions formed through blame and condemnation. Use forgiveness to let go. Stop carrying the past forward, shackled to your mind. Release the blame and let it return to the shadows of the past where it belongs. Only then will you be truly free and at peace.

Search your heart for any behavior or attitude that does not harmonize with forgiveness.

Sometimes we fool ourselves, believing we've forgiven someone when actually we're hiding behind our own sense of righteousness. Yet the stain of the rancor is actually visible through our words or actions. That's why it's essential to do an inner search for any residue that may linger.

Why be miserable when you can be happy? Liberate yourself from the chains of animosity by releasing your grievances once and for all. Forgive. Let go and live life with no regrets. Happiness is bound to follow!

# SECTION FOUR

# *Foraging in the Regions of Mind*

# Eight

# A Call to Action

*The road to hell is paved with good intentions.*
Proverb

## The Time is Now

Life doesn't offer guarantees. If you want or need something in your life to change, you can't sit back and expect, or even hope, that things will change for you. You have to be *pro*-active, not *re*-active to life.

Now is the time to discover the catalyst for changing your life. Usually it's a situation that provides the stimulus for change. Sometimes it's an internal discontent that spurs you to action. Can you pinpoint the incentive in your life? If not, no worries. Just the knowing that *something, anything* needs to change can be the impetus you need to get started.

At this point, you're probably asking yourself,

"Why is it necessary to identify *why* I want to change my life?" If you don't know your true motivation for inviting change into your life, you may miss important signposts. The essential reasons for transforming your life may slip by unnoticed. Then you may never uncover all the various elements that are actually obstructing your efforts. And you will miss important opportunities for self-discovery.

If you happen to be someone who knows definitively why you want or need to change, that's great. However, I would bet that if you wrote down your 'why' and free-associated a bit, you might turn up some additional, revealing details. (Don't you just love a good mystery?)

Picking up this book was your inner self's way of urging you to action. Not tomorrow or the next day. The future is only a distant dream, the past but a memory. *Now* is all that matters. Truly living in the present moment precludes the need to wallow in the past or project into the future. You can only live your life in the present moment, so why not begin this uniquely personal and spiritual journey *now*? Take the first steps down your Yellow Brick Road and see what exciting experiences, solutions and opportunities lie ahead!

# Self-Discovery: Questions & Answers

Now that you're familiar with the various

## Eight | A Call to Action

techniques presented in *The Little Guide*, a bit of inner searching needs to be attempted in order to find out the reasons you're holding yourself back from creating all the positive, life-affirming change you need and want in your life. Let's begin.

Find a quiet place where you will not be disturbed. Close your eyes. Calm and relax your body by slowing breathing in through your nostrils and out through your mouth. Inhale to a count of four, then hold the breath for a four count and finally exhale to another four count. Do this several times until you perceive the muscles in your body starting to unwind and relax. Do it a few more times until you feel centered and peaceful.

Now relax your mind by emptying out all stressful and insignificant thoughts. If harried or anxious notions are intruding, visualize a tranquil scene of nature. This could be the beauty of a mountain meadow filled with multi-colored flowers, their sweet perfume filling the air, or a canopy of trees creating a quiet respite from everyday stresses, or the soothing sound of the ocean on a warm summer's day. Whatever scene you imagine, be sure to include all the nuances that go with it: color, sound, smell, taste, touch, temperature, and don't forget any emotions that may arise.

Once you have finally calmed your thoughts and your body, and serenity has taken over, you are ready to look inside yourself and find the answers to what, where, when, why and how you hold yourself back from engaging in a vibrant life. Some questions to ask yourself to get to the root cause of your stagnation are as follows:

- *What do I want to change about my life?*
- *What's preventing me from changing this issue?*
- *What is the main obstacle that prevents me from living the life I've dreamed about?*
- *What other obstacles do I perceive as preventing me from changing my life?*
- *Are the barriers self-imposed or from outside myself?*
- *What main action is necessary for me to take control of my life?*
- *What other actions are required?*
- *What role do my thoughts play in limiting myself?*

  *My feelings?*

  *My words?*

  *My actions?*

- *Where do I hold myself back?*
- *Where do I hold myself back in relationships?*

  *In work relationships?*

  *In family relationships?*

  *In friendships?*

- *Are there certain situations or circumstances*

## Eight | A Call to Action

when I limit myself?
- When do I tend to limit myself most?
- How does my attitude toward myself prevent me from changing?
  My attitude toward others?
  My attitude toward work?
  My attitude toward marriage?
  My attitude toward my children?
  My attitude toward events or situations in my life?
- What adjustments in my attitude would be helpful?
- Why have I restricted myself?
- Why do I continue to restrict myself?
- Are there situations (or even people) in my life that are unhealthy for me and need changing?
- What qualities do I need to develop within myself that would be beneficial to changing my life?

Remember, the above questions are just a starting point. You may need to formulate questions unique to your particular situation.

As you ponder each question that seems relevant, allow any images to arise along with any subtlety of expression involving thoughts and feelings. Go with the first response that pops into your mind. Explore it by allowing the information to expand until you can clearly see the answer. It may come as a surprise, but stay with it. Oftentimes, the answer is quite illuminating! Self-discovery can be quite revealing and freeing, exposing the hidden elements of your psyche to the light of day. Treasure these moments as you uncover the real reasons you refrain from moving ahead and making changes in your life.

Take your time exploring these questions. This is not a process to be hurried through. Set aside a specific amount of time on a consistent basis to address these questions. Make sure you're thorough and find the answers to all the questions that pertain to your unique situation. This way, you'll be able to use your answers to formulate an action plan using some or all of the proven techniques discussed in *The Little Guide*. You'll then be able to focus on changing the issues that surfaced during your times of reflection.

## More Paths Along the Way

Contemplating the answers to self-directed questions is only one way to explore the reasons for your inertia. Journaling techniques, dream solutions, guided mental imagery and the use of drawings to express and explore feelings are equally valid methods for determining why your life has become fixed and immobile. Find the

### Eight | A Call to Action

method that works best for you and discover the reasons you've dug in your heels and simply won't move.

## Journaling

Journaling is a great way to uncover hidden obstructions and deterrents. Keeping a journal allows you to see the whole picture since at any time you can go back and read what was uppermost in your thoughts previously. You can really get a handle on how certain events and relationships have affected your life. It gives you a new and broader perspective of why things are the way they are and what steps you can take to motivate yourself in a new direction. If you find you can't write everyday, try for at least a few times a week. This will lend continuity to your journal and its contents will be more helpful to you overall.

What should you write about? Taking a cue from the questions in the previous section, examine the basis for your frustration with your life. Write about your feelings and thoughts in detail. What would you change if there were no restrictions? In what ways would your life be better? Writing allows you a safe way to explore what is hiding in your consciousness and is a great way to get to the heart of the matter.

You can also write extensively about the particular questions you've been contemplating.

After exploring one of the questions, write down your observations. Just don't write a synopsis of what occurred, but include all experiential details, as this will help you to remember the moment more easily when you review your writing. Then you can elaborate on your findings.

No matter which approach you take to get to the crux of the matter, write freely for as long as necessary without editing your thoughts. Allow yourself the freedom to express what is deep inside you. Write in an unguarded fashion, resisting the temptation to censor yourself. Liberate yourself from any restriction, knowing your journal is a private matter. This way you'll be comfortable with the process. Eventually, you'll want to go back and read what you've written. Put some distance between the writing phase and the time you go back to read your prose. This will give a fresh perspective on matters.

### *Dream Solutions*

When we sleep and head off into dreamtime, we give our body the opportunity to rest and replenish itself. However, there is so much more to dreaming than is immediately apparent. It is a great place to iron out the details of your life and for discovering your purpose for being born. When you start to stray from your intended mission, your nighttime dreams will clarify this. Unfortunately, so many disregard the importance

## Eight | A Call to Action

and relevance of dreaming. It's not about going on a mini vacation each night to la-la-land. It's the place where decisions are made and guidance can be sought.

Dreams can alert you when something is not right in your life, whether it's a relationship or a situation. Most people ignore how they feel in the morning, chalking up any lingering bad feelings to a terrible dream or nightmare. Your feelings are a clue and are one way your subconscious tries to get your attention.

When you need to discover what should change in your life, or how to begin changing your life, your dreams can supply the answer. Each night before you drift off to sleep, ask your question and request that you be shown, guided to or given the answer. This should be done nightly until you have your solution. Keeping a dream journal can be instrumental in discovering what you want to know; just don't forget to record your question as well.

If you're not remembering your dreams, don't get discouraged. Continue to ask that you be shown the answer. Eventually it will come, but patience is required. It may show up right before you awaken, in a pause between dreaming and wakefulness. This has sometimes been my experience.

No matter what your question or concern may be your subconscious will supply the answer. Dreams are one way for this to occur.

## Guided Imagery

There are some fun and creative ways using guided imagery that explore the hidden recesses of the mind. All involve use of the imagination. These techniques work best with another person but they can be done alone as well.

Write down a question you would like the answer to, but don't tell your partner. For example, "What type of work would I be happiest pursuing?" When you have finished writing down the question, immediately guide your partner using imagery to a point where his imagination will take over. For instance, tell him to visualize walking along a forest path, listening to the pleasant sounds of birds and other small creatures as he breathes in peace and contentment. Up ahead is a small clearing. When he reaches the edge of the clearing, he will see before him the answer to your question. He then verbally describes what he's seeing in all its detail. When he is finished, ask him to rate his vision on a scale of 1 to 10.

A variation of this method can be implemented when you're torn between two choices. You might ask, "Should I move to Chicago or Dallas"? The vision will contain elements of the appropriate choice. Even better ask, "How will I feel if I move to Dallas?" then, "How will I feel if I move to Chicago?" Again, write out the questions one at a time. Once you've written the first question,

## Eight | A Call to Action

initiate the guided imagery. Only move to the next question once your colleague has finished answering the first question completely, including the follow-up rating.

It's vitally important that your partner assign a value to his impressions before letting him in on what question he was answering. And if he's answering a series of questions, don't reveal them until he's completely finished. On the scale of 1 to 10, eight and above should be taken as very positive, seven as just okay and below that you might want to reevaluate your choices. You may find that somewhere else altogether would be a better match for you.

Instead of using the imagery of a forest and a clearing, you can direct your partner to visualizing a single door, which he subsequently opens, describing the scene in front of him. If you ask a question that involves choices, have him visualize the required number of doors and he decides which one to open. For example, if you ask, "Should I move to Miami, Phoenix or Seattle?" guide him to three doors and tell him to choose the best one. Have him describe what he sees when he opens the door and then rate his choice. Only reveal the question after he's completely finished. Again, it's entirely possible that none is right for you.

No matter what guided imagery you use, always have your partner rate his vision. This gives invaluable information about his foresight. And feel free to change the imagery to something of your own choosing.

If you want to try doing this alone, I suggest you write down several questions at once, folding each question so it can fit in the palm of your hand. Mix them up in a hat or some other container and draw one. Without looking at the question, hold it in your hand and proceed with the guided imagery of your choice. Afterwards, remember to rate it. Write down your responses, keeping the folded question with the appropriate response. Then proceed to the next question and so on and so forth. Once you're completely finished with the visions, the rating and written responses, then look to see what question you answered along with reviewing your response. It can be quite revealing!

Guided imagery can really speed up the responses from your subconscious and the rating system adds another important dimension to the work. It can clue you into whether or not a choice you are considering is really appropriate for you. Use the guided imagery with the art technique described below for added measure, or substitute drawing for the written responses altogether.

## *Using Art*

Art is another way to explore what's keeping you from changing the things in your life that aren't working. Even if you don't feel you have any artistic talent you can still express yourself with abstract art. Drawing or painting can be an outlet for communicating difficult emotions. Often, people don't have outlets for their pent up creativity. Everyone is so busy throughout the day that unless you're in an artistic field, chances are you don't have an outlet to express yourself. Drawing or painting in an abstract manner frees you to accept the boundless and unknown. There are no rules to follow, no special techniques required; only the use of your imagination is necessary.

Focus on any feeling you might have trouble expressing or go back to the questions addressed earlier in the chapter, selecting one that resonates with you. Use that feeling or question to get to the root of any block you might be experiencing and with pencil or paintbrush in hand, express yourself with whatever symbols, images and colors will convey their meaning. This should loosen the encumbrance enough that with a bit more inner searching you will find the answer you've been seeking.

# Self-Direction

Once you've chosen how to unlock the factors that may be holding you back, beginning with the single most important thing you would like to change, write down an action plan using the methods found in *The Little Guide*. Make sure it is a doable plan you can and will implement. Writing it down makes it more tangible and can be helpful in focusing your efforts.

Perhaps working on forgiveness is the solution to healing that once important relationship; include visualization for added emphasis. Maybe meditation in conjunction with introspection is the best alternative for eliminating that stubborn character flaw. On the other hand, visualization and prayer along with some positivity could be just the thing you need to develop the courage and fortitude to take action in some endeavor, for example, opening your own business.

Whatever action plan you choose, you may find it helpful to revisit your plan occasionally to keep yourself on track, for fine-tuning or to gauge just how far you've come. After a while, you will add more pieces (issues, problems or areas of life to change) to your daily action plan, but do so slowly so you're not overwhelmed. And remember to embrace those four important attributes discussed in chapter one: patience, courage, persistence and belief in yourself.

All changes begin with one small step. Change only one thing about you or your situation. Master it to where you have infused your consciousness with it, so it is truly a part of you. Then move to the next small step. With focus and determination

## Eight | A Call to Action

you will soon be on your way to moving forward with your life. The changes will come upon you in subtle ways and before you know it, your issue, your situation, your self will be different. Your life will be transformed!

# Source Notes

## Choose Change

Henry David Thoreau, www.QuotationsPage.com

Jesus said these words: Matthew 7:7, New International Bible Version. www.BibleGateway.com

## Speaking from the Heart

Mahatma Gandhi, www.WorldOfQuotes.com

David R. Hawkins, M.D., PhD, *Dialogues on Consciousness and Spirituality* (1997), p.8.

John Van Auken, *Power of Prayer* article, online Personal Spirituality newsletter www.edgarcayce.org/ps/powerofprayer.html

Why worry when you can pray: Edgar Cayce Reading 2528-2, Edgar Cayce Readings © 1971, 1993, - 2009 by the Edgar Cayce Foundation. All rights reserved.

live the way you pray: Edgar Cayce Reading 5758-1, *ibid*.

## Whispers of the One

*Edgar Cayce* Reading 3226-2, *ibid*.

chakras correspond to the endocrine system: Edgar Cayce Reading 262-127, *ibid*.

glands of the body are gateways: Edgar Cayce Reading 281-38, *ibid*.

head and neck exercise: Edgar Cayce Reading 2982-2, *ibid*.

ideals: Edgar Cayce Readings, *ibid.*
Spirit is the life: Edgar Cayce Reading 254-42, *ibid.*

## Looking Within

Aldous Huxley, www.WisdomQuotes.com
each thought and emotion: The teachings of Dr. Stylianos Atteshlis, www.Daskalos.org
thought forms can never be erased: *ibid.*
cleansing the personality: *ibid.*
Introspection: *ibid.*

## Seeing is Creating

Albert Einstein, www.QuotationsPage.com
Goethe, Johann Wolfgang von, *Faust*, transl. by John Anster. London: Cassell, 835, page 20. See also www.goethe.de/ins/gb/lon/wis/rec/kur/enindex.htm
gold is the true color of healing: Dr. Kenneth Y. Davis and Lisa V. Davis, co-founders of Natural Force Healing®, Advanced Practitioner's Course, 10/98.

## Life Approach

Ralph Waldo Emerson, Susan Hayward, *A Guide for the Advanced Soul* (1984).

## Freedom is Yours

Norman Cousins, www.QuotationsPage.com
holding onto resentment: Edgar Cayce Readings, Edgar Cayce Readings © 1971, 1993, -2009 by the Edgar Cayce Foundation. All rights reserved.

not all illness is the result: Dr. Kenneth Y. Davis and Lisa V. Davis, co-founders of Natural Force Healing®, Phase I workshop, 1995.

Forgiveness Prayer: Dr. Kenneth Y. Davis, co-founder of Natural Force Healing®, www.naturalforcehealing.com

## A Call to Action

*Proverb*, www.answers.com/topic/list-of-english-proverbs

## Recommended Readings

*The Holographic Universe* by Michael Talbot

*Power vs Force* by David R. Hawkins, MD, PhD

*Transcending the Levels of Consciousness* by David R. Hawkins, MD, PhD

*Dialogues on Consciousness and Spirituality* by David R. Hawkins, MD, PhD

*The Art of Happiness* by The Dalai Lama

*To Love Is to Be Happy With* by Barry Neil Kaufman

*A Guide for the Advanced Soul* by Susan Hayward

*The Magus of Strovolos* by Kyriacos C. Markides

*Homage to the Sun* by Kyriacos C. Markides

*Fire in the Heart* by Kyriacos C. Markides

*The Seat of the Soul* by Gary Zukav

*The Heart of the Soul* by Gary Zukav

*The Second Coming of Christ, Vol. 1 & 2* by Paramahansa Yogananda

*Many Mansions* by Gina Cerminara

*Edgar Cayce's Story of Karma* by Mary Ann Woodward

*The Edgar Cayce Companion* by B. Ernest Frejer

*What Color is Your Parachute* by Richard Nelson Bolles

# About the Author

Sarah M. Collins is a prolific writer, award-winning author and alternative health expert. She has been active in the alternative healthcare movement since 1995 as a natural health practitioner and consultant. She enjoys writing about alternative health & wellness and issues dealing with spirituality, often combining the two topics as there is a dynamic link between these two fields. In addition, Sarah is a frequent contributor to MARCI, an online magazine of the Holistic Mentorship Network.

Her lifelong studies in metaphysics and personal development have culminated in her first published book *The Little Guide to Big Changes: 6 Steps to Creating Lasting, Positive Change in Your Life*. The book is the award winner (self-help category) of the 2010 International Book Awards.

Sarah is available for speaking engagements on health and/or spirituality. Please send any inquiries to:

sarah@wellnesscaretoday.com

# THE POWER OF NEW ATTITUDE

Foreword by:
John C. Maxwell

**Dr. Alan E. Nelson**

ISBN-13 : 978-93-806190-6-4
**First Good Times Edition 2010**

When you want so much to succeed,
**why are you often disappointed?**

If your heart's in the right place,
**why do you keep getting hurt?**

You may be your own worst enemy—
**without even knowing it.**

Dr. Alan E. Nelson counsels people every year to help them recognize the behaviors and attitudes that defeat them. *The Power of a New Attitude* explores nineteen of the most common "behavitudes"—behaviors that stem from wrong attitudes—and helps you evaluate your own life to identify and change self-defeating behaviors. With this book's helpful insights, you can achieve your goals and live the successful life you long for.

# THE POWER OF POSITIVE LIVING

THE POWER WITHIN YOU

**G.C. Beri**

ISBN-13 : 978-81-909396-8-3
**First South Asian Edition 2010**

This book brings out very effectively the significance of positive attitude in moulding one's life for success and happiness. It provides guidance to an aspiring reader who may not be happy with his present position but is ambitious to be an achiever in life.

A distinguishing feature of the book is that it not only emphasizes the need for a balanced life but also suggests methods by which one can integrate worldly progress with spiritual awakening.

The book is sprinkled with live examples and the words of wisdom drawn from varied sources. In addition, it has a lucid exposition and as the reader goes through its chapters, he will feel motivated to bring about a significant transformation in his life.

www.goodtimesbooks.com

Have you enjoyed the book?
We hope this book has helped you in
**Rediscovering The New World**

Join us on facebook
www.facebook.com/Good.Times.Books